Backyard
**Bugs**
&Creepy-
Crawlies

# Worms

**Victoria Hazlehurst**

Explore other books at:
WWW.ENGAGEBOOKS.COM

VANCOUVER, B.C.

e→ WWW.ENGAGEBOOKS.COM

*Worms: Level Pre-1*
*Backyard Bugs & Creepy Crawlies*
Roscoe-Roumanis, Victoria 1945 –
Text © 2022 Engage Books
Design © 2022 Engage Books

Edited by: A.R. Roumanis
and Sarah Harvey

Text set in Epilogue

FIRST EDITION / FIRST PRINTING

LIBRARY AND ARCHIVES CANADA CATALOGUING IN PUBLICATION

Title: Worms / Victoria Roscoe-Roumanis.
Names: Roscoe-Roumanis, Victoria, author.
Description: Series statement: Backyard bugs & creepy-crawlies
Engaging readers: level pre-1, beginner.

Identifiers: Canadiana (print) 2022040349X | Canadiana (ebook) 20220403503
ISBN 978-1-77476-720-7 (hardcover)
ISBN 978-1-77476-721-4 (softcover)
ISBN 978-1-77476-722-1 (epub)
ISBN 978-1-77476-723-8 (pdf)

Subjects:
LCSH: Worms—Juvenile literature.

Classification: LCC QL386.6 .R68 2022 | DDC J592/.3—DC23

This project has been made possible in part
by the Government of Canada.

Canada ⁂

Worms are great
for gardens.

3

Worms have no arms or legs.

They move around using their strong muscles.

Tiny hairs help worms hold onto the soil around them.

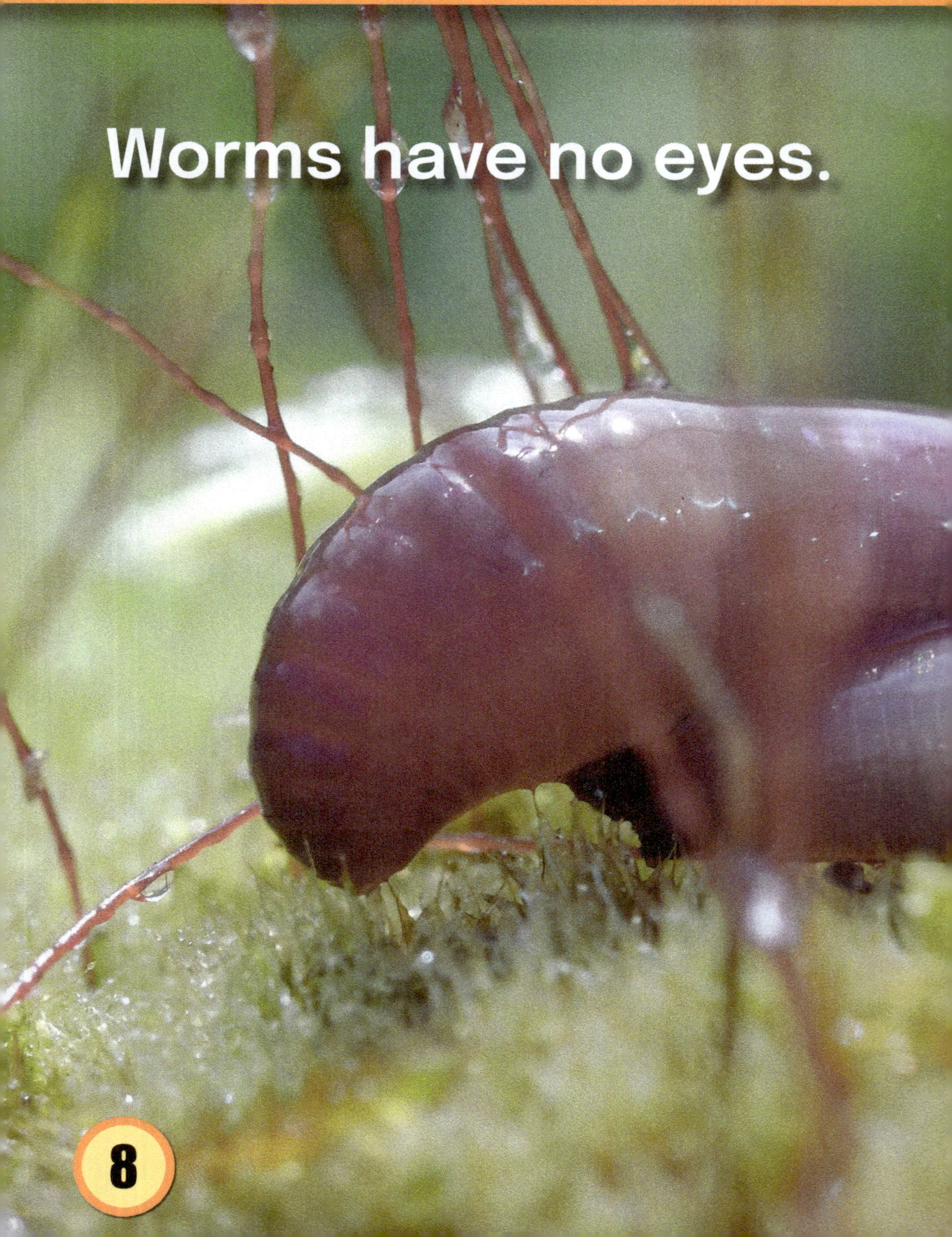

Worms have no eyes.

They sense light
through their skin.

Too much light is
not good for them.

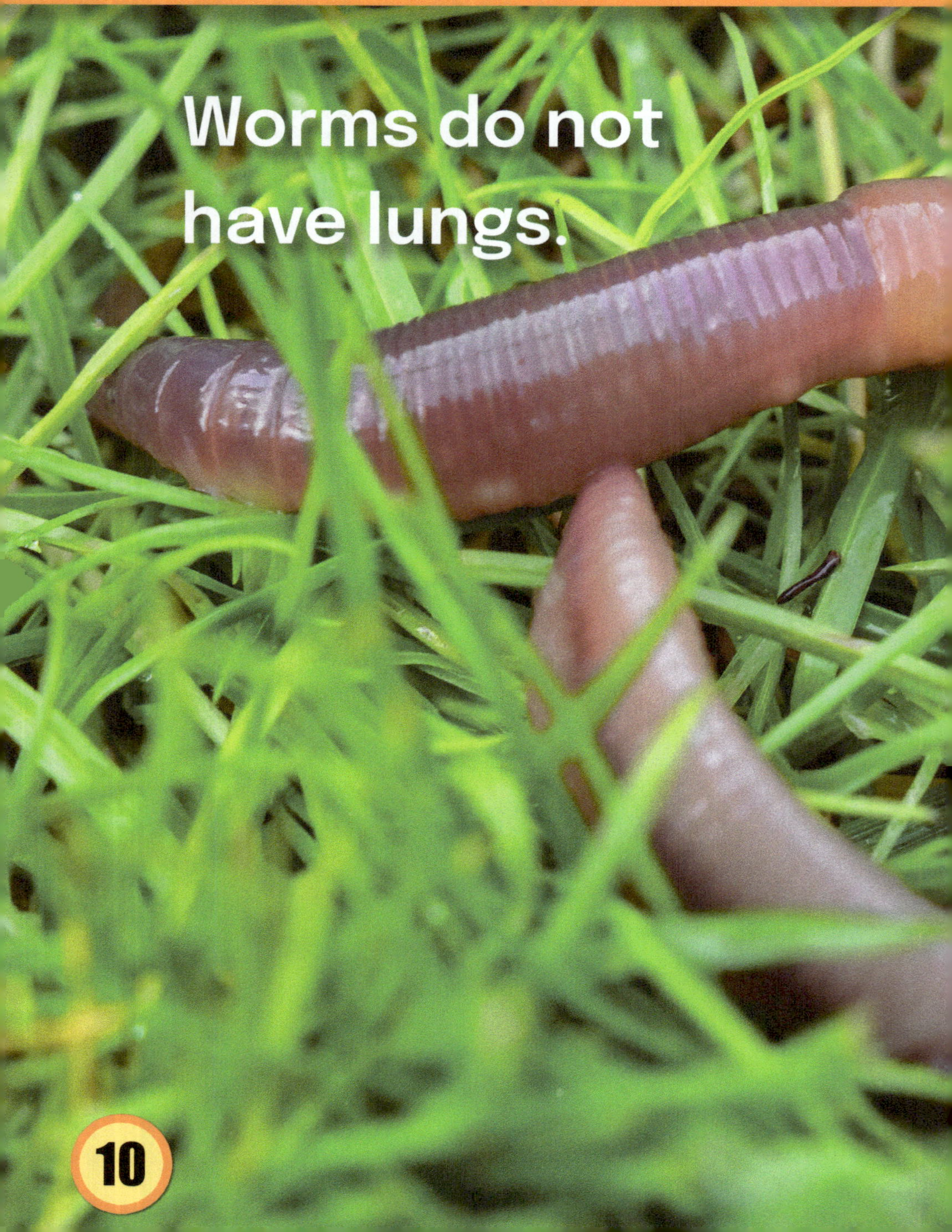

Worms do not have lungs.

They breathe
through their skin.

11

Worms have
five hearts.

Their hearts are close
to their mouths.

Mouth

Worms make
tunnels in soil.

Tunnels bring water and air into the ground.

To make tunnels,
worms eat dirt.

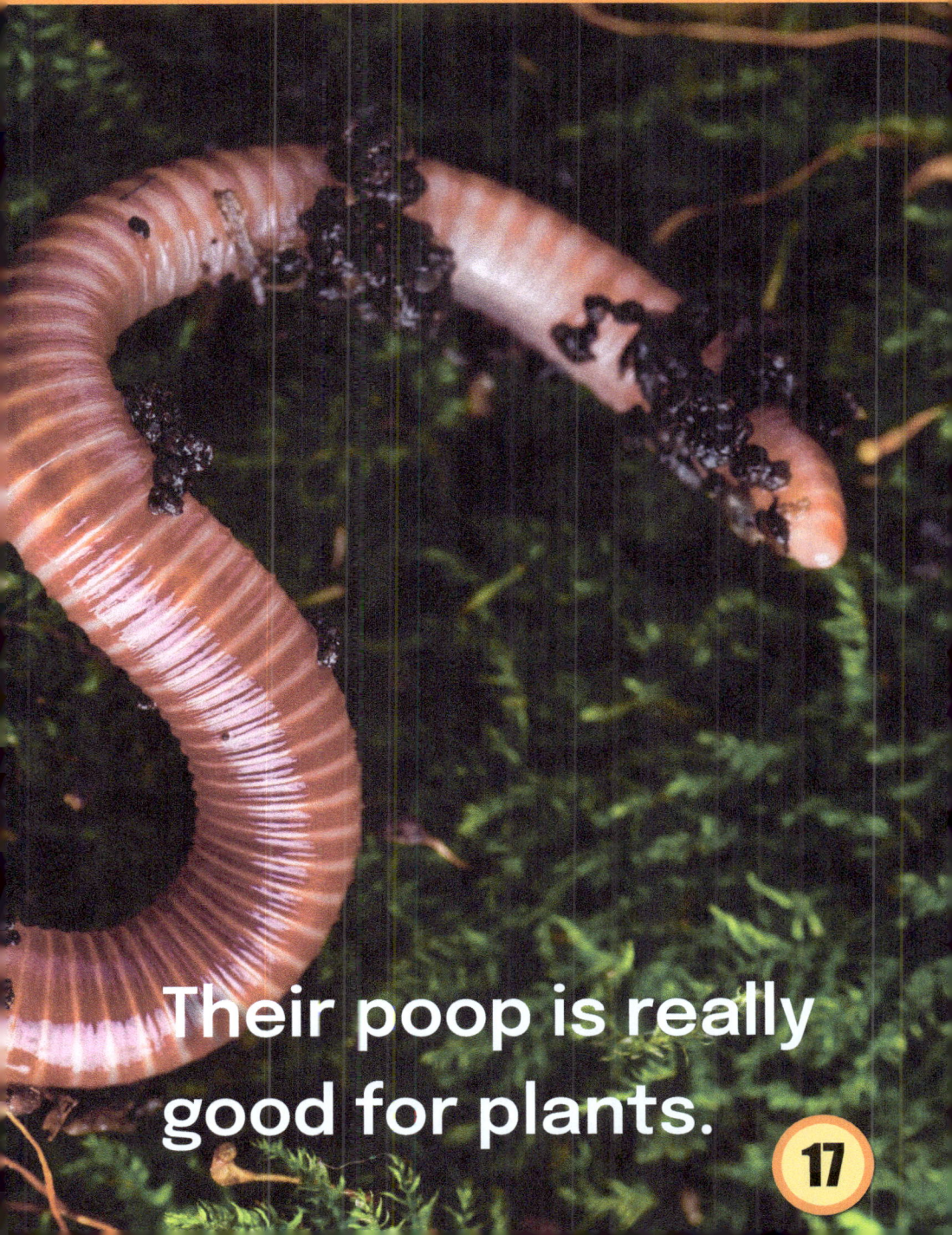

Their poop is really good for plants.

Worms need to keep their skin wet.

If a worm's skin dries out, it will die.

Worms feed on dead plants and animals.

They will also
eat paper and
coffee beans.

Baby worms hatch from cocoons smaller than a grain of rice.

**Cocoon**

Each cocoon can have 1 to 20 eggs in it.

Some worms live in
the ocean.

24

The bearded fireworm can sting other animals.

Worms are
an important
food source.

Birds, frogs, and fish all eat worms.

Please put me back in the dirt! I like it there.

29

# Explore other books in the Backyard Bugs & Creepy Crawlies series!

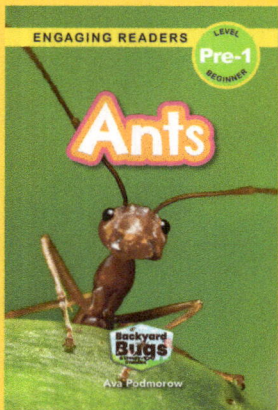

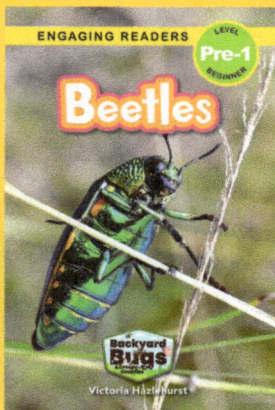

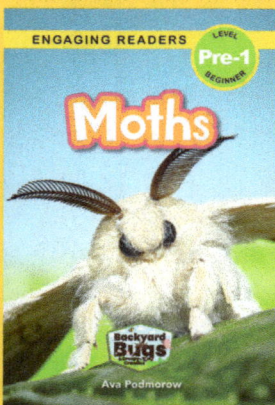

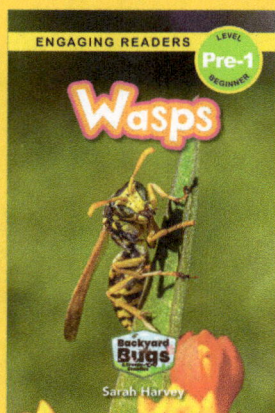

Visit www.engagebooks.com/readers

# Explore books in the Animals In The City series.

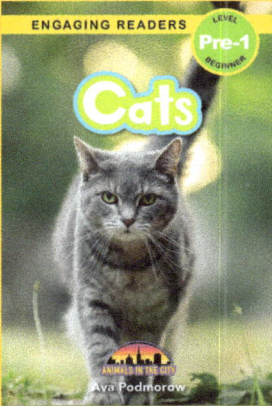

ENGAGING READERS — LEVEL Pre-1 BEGINNER
**Cats**
ANIMALS IN THE CITY
Ava Podmorow

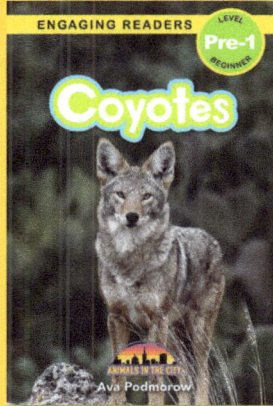

ENGAGING READERS — LEVEL Pre-1 BEGINNER
**Coyotes**
ANIMALS IN THE CITY
Ava Podmorow

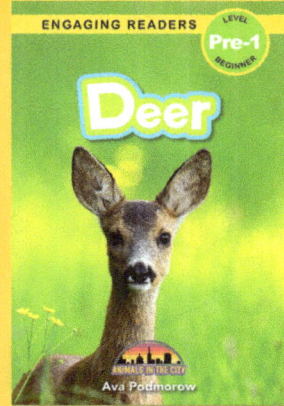

ENGAGING READERS — LEVEL Pre-1 BEGINNER
**Deer**
ANIMALS IN THE CITY
Ava Podmorow

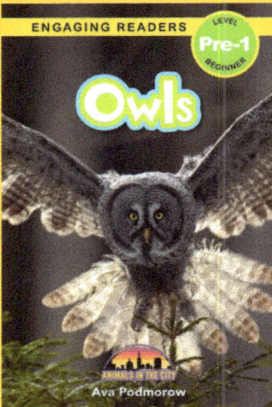

ENGAGING READERS — LEVEL Pre-1 BEGINNER
**Owls**
ANIMALS IN THE CITY
Ava Podmorow

ENGAGING READERS — LEVEL Pre-1 BEGINNER
**Pigeons**
ANIMALS IN THE CITY
Ava Podmorow

ENGAGING READERS — LEVEL Pre-1 BEGINNER
**Rabbits**
ANIMALS IN THE CITY
Ava Podmorow

ENGAGING READERS — LEVEL Pre-1 BEGINNER
**Raccoons**
ANIMALS IN THE CITY
Sarah Harvey

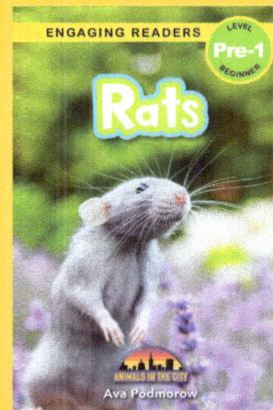

ENGAGING READERS — LEVEL Pre-1 BEGINNER
**Rats**
ANIMALS IN THE CITY
Ava Podmorow

ENGAGING READERS — LEVEL Pre-1 BEGINNER
**Skunks**
ANIMALS IN THE CITY
Ava Podmorow

Visit www.engagebooks.com/readers

www.ingramcontent.com/pod-product-compliance
Lightning Source LLC
Chambersburg PA
CBHW051241020426
42331CB00016B/3479